AIR FORCE CAREERS

CYNTHIA O'BRIEN

CAREERS ON THE FRONT LINE

CRABTREE
PUBLISHING COMPANY
WWW.CRABTREEBOOKS.COM

CRABTREE
PUBLISHING COMPANY
WWW.CRABTREEBOOKS.COM

Author: Cynthia O'Brien
Editors: Sarah Eason
 Jennifer Sanderson
 Ellen Rodger
Proofreader: Tracey Kelly
Indexer: Tracey Kelly
Editorial director:
 Kathy Middleton
Interior design: Emma DeBanks
Cover and logo design:
 Katherine Berti
Photo research: Rachel Blount
Print coordinator:
 Katherine Berti
Consultant: David Hawksett

Written, developed, and produced for Crabtree
 Publishing by Calcium Creative Ltd.

Photo Credits:
t=Top, tr=Top Right, tl=Top Left
Inside: Shutterstock: BlueBarronPhoto: p. 29; Anurake
Singto-On: p. 28t; Joseph Sohm: p. 28b; U.S. Air Force:
Joshua Armstrong: p. 7; Tech. Sgt. Gregory Brook: pp.
3, 9; James M. Bowman: p. 4; Tech. Sgt. Keith Brown:
p. 11; Airman 1st Class Michael S. Dorus: p. 21; Senior
Airman Travis Edwards: p. 25; Airman 1st Class Ericka
Engblom: p. 12; Tech. Sgt. James L. Harper Jr.: pp. 1,
24; Tech. Sgt. Robert Horstman: p. 5; Staff. Sgt. Adawn
Kelsey: p. 17; Samuel King Jr.: p. 20; Senior Airman
Robert L. McIlrath: p. 27; Capt. Victoria Porto: p. 13;
Senior Airman Andrea Posey: p. 19; Courtesy photo by
Master Sgt. Ivan Ruiz: p. 15; Brad White: p. 8; Staff Sgt.
Taylor Worley: p. 6; U.S. Navy: Mass Communication
Specialist 2nd Class Christopher Lange: p. 23;
Wikimedia Commons: U.S. Air Force photo by Staff
Sgt. Kelly Goonan: p. 16. Front cover: Shutterstock

Library and Archives Canada Cataloguing in Publication

Title: Air force careers / Cynthia O'Brien.
Names: O'Brien, Cynthia (Cynthia J.), author.
Description: Series statement: Careers on the front line |
 Includes bibliographical references and index.
Identifiers: Canadiana (print) 20200283839 |
 Canadiana (ebook) 20200283847 |
 ISBN 9780778781370 (hardcover) |
 ISBN 9780778781431 (softcover) |
 ISBN 9781427125774 (HTML)
Subjects: LCSH: United States. Air Force—Vocational
 guidance—Juvenile literature. | LCSH: United
 States. Air Force—Recruiting, enlistment, etc.—
 Juvenile literature. | LCSH: Canada. Royal
 Canadian Air Force—Vocational guidance—Juvenile
 literature. | LCSH: Canada. Royal Canadian Air
 Force—Recruiting, enlistment, etc.—Juvenile literature.
Classification: LCC UG631 .O27 2020 | DDC j358.40023—dc23

Library of Congress Cataloging-in-Publication Data

Names: O'Brien, Cynthia (Cynthia J.) author.
Title: Air force careers / Cynthia O'Brien.
Description: New York : Crabtree Publishing Company, [2021]
 | Series: Careers on the front line | Includes index.
Identifiers: LCCN 2020029754 (print) |
 LCCN 2020029755 (ebook) |
 ISBN 9780778781370 (hardcover) |
 ISBN 9780778781431 (paperback) |
 ISBN 9781427125774 (ebook)
Subjects: LCSH: United States. Air Force--Vocational guidance-
 -Juvenile literature. | United States. Air Force--Juvenile
 literature. | Airmen--United States--Juvenile literature.
Classification: LCC UG633 .O24 2021 (print) |
 LCC UG633 (ebook) | DDC 358.40023--dc23
LC record available at https://lccn.loc.gov/2020029754
LC ebook record available at https://lccn.loc.gov/2020029755

Crabtree Publishing Company
www.crabtreebooks.com   1-800-387-7650

Printed in the U.S.A./082020/CG20200710

Published in Canada
Crabtree Publishing
616 Welland Ave.
St. Catharines, Ontario
L2M 5V6

Published in the United States
Crabtree Publishing
347 Fifth Ave
Suite 1402-145
New York, NY 10016

Published in the United Kingdom
Crabtree Publishing
Maritime House
Basin Road North, Hove
BN41 1WR

Published in Australia
Crabtree Publishing
3 Charles Street
Coburg North
VIC, 3058

CONTENTS

DEFENSE IN THE AIR

Countries around the world have military, or armed, forces that defend their nations. An air force is one of a country's most important armed forces, together with the navy and the army. The Royal Canadian Air Force formed in 1924. In the United States, the Air Force became a military branch separate to the rest of the U.S. armed forces in 1947. Today, the U.S. Air Force has more than 5,000 aircraft, including bombers and fighters. It has the largest number of aircraft in the world and is the most advanced air force.

REACHING FOR THE SKIES

The U.S. Air Force has more than 328,000 active duty members and nearly 70,000 reserves, who are part-time. Active duty members serve the Air Force full time and may be **deployed** anywhere in the world. Most reserves work one weekend per month and two full weeks every year. They work for Air Force units close to home. Some may have a **civilian** job or be a student at college or university. Reserves can also be called to active duty if the Air Force needs them. Whatever path people choose, those in the U.S. Air Force must pass the Armed Services Vocational **Aptitude** Battery (ASVAB). The Canadian Air Force has the Canadian Forces Aptitude Test (CFAT). Both tests ensure that candidates are suited to the Air Force.

In the U.S. Air Force, it is the tradition that, regardless of gender, all members are called "airmen."

Airmen prepare a B-52 aircraft for takeoff. The bomber can fly 8,800 miles (14,162 km) without refueling.

BASIC TRAINING

After passing the ASVAB test, all new recruits go through the Air Force's basic training. This is eight and a half weeks of testing and learning. Physical training is just a part of the overall course. There are classes in leadership and **ethics**, and an introduction to **nuclear** warfare. During the fourth week, cadets go through a **tactical** course and do **security** training. To be successful, trainees have to be willing to learn, be **disciplined**, and work as a team.

Your FRONTLINE Career

Look for "Your Frontline Career" boxes. They highlight the skills and strengths needed for specific Air Force careers. They can be used to help you decide whether a career in the Air Force is for you and what roles might suit you best.

FRONTLINE AIR FORCE

Being part of the Air Force means joining a specialized team. In the United States, this will be one of the ten major commands, or divisions, of the Air Force. The Air Combat Command, Air Force Global Strike Command, and Air Force Special Operations Command are three of the commands that provide Air Force power in times of conflict. Each command has numbered air units within it, and each numbered unit has a particular focus of duty. The Royal Canadian Air Force operates 14 wings, or units, of command. Within the wings are smaller units called squadrons.

CHAIN OF COMMAND

The U.S. Air Force divisions have specific missions, but all of them work together. The Air Force follows a strict **chain of command**. **Enlisted** basic airmen are the lowest **rank**. **Commissioned** officers start out as Second Lieutenants. Squadron Commanders report to Wing Commanders. Above these ranks are the heads of the major commands. They report to the Chief of Staff of the Air Force. The Chief of Staff of the Air Force falls under the Secretary of the Air Force, who reports to the U.S. Secretary of Defense. The Secretary of Defense reports to the President of the United States.

Airmen receive a new badge called an insignia as they rise through the ranks. This airman is receiving a Master Sergeant insignia to mark the new position.

*Some Air Force cadets work on projects involving **satellites** and oversee their launches.*

READY FOR COMBAT

Air Combat is the largest of the commands and provides a huge range of services. It trains and equips forces and operates about 1,000 aircraft. The training includes preparing airmen for air, **cyberspace**, and **intelligence** missions. Special Operations commands go wherever they are needed. They take part in combat, **reconnaissance**, and other vital tasks. The Air Force Global Strike Command (AFGSC) was formed in 2009 and oversees most of the U.S. Air Force's nuclear weapons. Its fleet of bomber aircraft can carry out nuclear or **conventional** strikes. However, the AFGSC also prevents attacks on the United States by land or air. The Nuclear Command, Control and Communications (NC3) Center, part of the AFGSC, is a central unit that provides intelligence and an important link between the government and nuclear armed forces.

SPACE COMMAND

In December 2019, the U.S. Space Force officially became the sixth branch of the U.S. military. Some of the Space Force's duties include controlling satellites, monitoring the space activities of other countries, and guarding against **ballistic missile** launches.

FRONTLINE PILOTS

Pilots in the Air Force fly some of the most advanced aircraft in the world. These highly trained and skilled officers take charge of fighters, bombers, transportation planes, and tankers. They also control unmanned aerial vehicles (UAVs), which are remotely controlled aircraft. In the U.S. Air Force, there are about 12,500 pilots. Combat pilots may drop bombs, shoot missiles, or shoot down enemy missiles. However, pilots take on many other missions, such as dropping off supplies to troops on the ground or those in a **humanitarian crisis**.

GETTING THEIR WINGS

Recruits need a college or university degree to train as a pilot. A science or engineering degree provides a good background for work as a pilot. Having some civilian pilot training is also a good idea. Once candidates have passed officer testing and training, they go on to have specialized flight training. This takes a year of classroom lessons and **virtual reality** flights that lead to in-flight lessons. The next step is learning how to fly specific aircraft. The best trainees also have excellent physical fitness and eyesight. At graduation, U.S. and Canadian Air Force pilots receive their wings badge.

*Fighter pilots wear special clothes to protect them from gravity forces, as well as chemical or **biological** attacks.*

Before takeoff, pilots check the aircraft equipment to make sure that everything is working properly.

FLYING FOR THE FORCE

Flying for the Air Force is exciting and a great opportunity to see the world. It may mean serving in combat zones, but it also means being able to help in disasters. Air Force pilots are part of an important and respected service. However, this job also can involve long tours of duty and being stationed far from home.

FLYING MISSIONS

Air Force pilots are deployed across North America. U.S. pilots are also **stationed** at **bases** around the world. Pilots have different jobs, depending on the command and the aircraft they fly. The Air Force assigns new pilots to a squadron within one of the major commands. They learn how to use all of the **navigation**, communications, and weapons systems on board the aircraft. All pilots also have ground duties, such as planning and tactical training, as well as flight exercises to do when they are not on a mission.

Major Mary Jennings Hegar:
RESCUE UNDER FIRE

On July 29, 2009, the mission was clear: Three U.S. soldiers lay injured from an explosion in Afghanistan. They needed immediate rescue. Helicopter pilot Major Mary Jennings Hegar and her copilot flew near the scene and saw a line of U.S. Army trucks. However, about 150 **Taliban** soldiers were hiding nearby. Seconds later, bullets began to fly.

Your FRONTLINE Career

Is Being a Helicopter Pilot for You?

Sounds Great
- Traveling around the world
- Flying the latest, most powerful helicopters
- Taking part in intelligence and combat missions
- Helping people in natural disasters

Things to Think About
- May be stationed in remote places
- Must commit to ten years of active duty service
- May be part of dangerous missions
- Pilots must have excellent vision and no history of asthma or allergies

The Taliban blasted through the helicopter windshield, hitting Hegar in the arm and thigh. She returned fire while she and the copilot landed the helicopter. The enemy fire became intense, and Hegar stood by with a rifle. She protected the **pararescue** team as they carried the injured soldiers to the helicopter. With her helicopter loaded but damaged, Hegar took off again before having to make an emergency landing in the hills. Two U.S. Army helicopters arrived in the nick of time to take the team and the injured to safety.

Years before this terrifying episode, Hegar was a young girl who dreamed about flying. As she grew older, she focused on a career in the military. When Hegar was in high school, she applied to attend the Air Force Reserve Officer Training Corps (AFROTC). A high school teacher's comment about women having no place in the military just made her more determined. The next summer, she started her training.

During her first job, Hegar worked on aircraft maintenance in Japan. As a woman, she faced more **discrimination** there but found encouragement, too.

Hegar fought hard for women such as these airmen to be allowed more combat roles. In 2013, the U.S. government opened up more positions to female airmen.

By 2001, she had her pilot's license, and a few years later, she became a pilot for the Air National Guard. This is a reserve branch of the U.S. Air Force that carries out missions at home and overseas. The Air National Guard must be ready for active duty at any time.

In 2009, Hegar was in Afghanistan on her third tour. Hegar's actions on that fateful day in July saved the lives of her crew and the three injured soldiers. Later that year, the military awarded her the Purple Heart, an honor for military **personnel** wounded at war. She also received other awards, including the Distinguished Flying Cross with Valor. Hegar's injuries ended her flying career, but she continues to fight for women's rights in the military and to encourage women to enlist. In 2017, Hegar published a book about her amazing experiences in the military, entitled *Shoot Like a Girl*.

AIR FORCE SPECIAL OPS

When war rages or natural disasters strike, the experts from the Air Force Special Operations Command are there to help. The command is ready to fly out if there is a need for **precision** air strikes during a conflict. The Air Force Special Operations Command also has specialists who rescue people in combat zones. They may be deployed anywhere in the world at any time.

READY FOR ANYTHING

It takes fierce determination to be part of the Air Force Special Operations Command. The training is very tough. After basic training, it takes many more weeks and testing to make it into the Special Operations Command. These trainees learn parachuting, diving, and mountaineering skills. They also go through survival school, which is a course that teaches them how to survive in all conditions. Special Ops forces may land anywhere, from hot, dry deserts to jungles, so they need to know how to survive in any situation.

The Royal Canadian Air Force does not have a separate Special Operations branch. Instead, the Joint Task Force 2 (JTF 2) is a Special Ops force that recruits from all branches of the armed forces. The focus of this unit is **counterterrorism**, but it also supplies security forces in special situations. It is on hand for any threat to Canadians at home or overseas.

Special Ops forces are armed and ready to shoot to protect other aircrew and aircraft.

COMBAT OPERATION AND CONTROL

It takes a lot of planning and coordination to carry out air combat missions. The U.S. Special Ops Command deploys combat controllers into conflict zones. In these dangerous positions, the controllers find airfields, manage air traffic, and help to direct the action. They have to do all of this covertly, or secretly, and may have to deal with enemy forces at any time.

*Air Force weather teams use balloons to test weather conditions in **hostile** areas.*

MORE THAN THE WEATHER

*Knowing about the weather can mean the difference between whether a military operation fails or succeeds. Special Reconnaissance airmen work day or night in any climate. As part of Special Ops, they operate in hostile areas and have combat training. They are also skilled **meteorologists**. Military planning depends on the environmental data, or information, they supply.*

Master Sergeant Ivan Ruiz:
PARARESCUE HERO

In the early morning of December 10, 2013, Chinook helicopters hovered near the village of Mushan in Afghanistan. It was still dark. Quietly, they dropped Master Sergeant Ivan Ruiz (a U.S. Air Force pararescue specialist), a 12-person team of U.S. Army forces, and a number of **allied** Afghan fighters. The joint forces were there to clear the village of Taliban fighters and their weapons. Bullets started flying as soon as Ruiz and the soldiers hit the ground.

Your FRONTLINE Career

Is Being a Pararescue Specialist for You?

Sounds Great
- Exciting, important missions
- Saving lives
- Job combines combat and medical duties
- Working with other forces in the military

Things to Think About
- At the front line of danger
- Must be ready to go anywhere in the world at a moment's notice
- Very tough, long training that is difficult to pass
- Must be excellent at many tasks, including diving, swimming, parachuting, and weaponry

Attack helicopters fired back and cleared the way for the joint forces to move forward. Then, just as they neared the Taliban **compound**, they faced more gunfire from the top of the building. Ruiz and the other Americans split up to surround the compound. Some of the U.S. soldiers moved into the courtyard, an open area inside. Ruiz and his team stood guard by the door, while the soldiers made it to the main building. Ruiz and two other soldiers crept forward into the courtyard toward small huts.

Suddenly, enemy fire caught one of the soldiers with Ruiz. More bullets shot out from the huts and hit the other soldier. Ruiz was caught in an open space, firing back at the gunfire still blasting from the huts.

Ruiz knew he needed to move his wounded teammates to safety, but the gunfire did not stop. With the help of another soldier providing cover, Ruiz crawled to the injured soldiers. But the Taliban then threw out **grenades**, and the third grenade sent the soldier who was covering Ruiz flying into the air. Thankfully, he survived.

Meanwhile, an allied Afghan fighter and more U.S. soldiers arrived as backup and started firing on the Taliban. Finally, Ruiz pulled the two soldiers to safety, so that he could give them emergency medical treatment. Then, he took them to the **evacuation** helicopter and went back inside the compound to help finish the fight.

Ruiz has emergency medical training as well as arms and intense physical training. He needed to use all of these skills when he was caught in combat.

COMBAT SYSTEMS OFFICERS

Combat Systems Officers (CSOs) are mission commanders. They plan Air Force operations and direct airmen during missions. They use the latest equipment to control weapon, navigation, and **electronic warfare** systems. They also support Special Forces troops on the ground.

TRAINED TO BE THE BEST

Like all officers, CSOs need a degree. Degrees in engineering, physical sciences, such as chemistry, or mathematics help give future CSOs a solid base for their Air Force training. CSO training is an intense, year-long process. Trainees learn about **meteorology**, navigation, aircraft guidance, and weapons systems. The training is in a classroom and in aircraft, and includes **simulated** flying. After graduating, CSOs must commit to six years of service. The Air Force assigns them to squadrons and types of aircraft, from training and rescue teams to bombers and fighters. After this, there is more training so that CSOs develop the specific skills they need.

MISSION CONTROL

There are no missions that CSOs cannot handle. For example, they are involved in anti-submarine operations and stopping suspected **piracy**. They manage search-and-rescue missions, even in enemy territories. They do **surveillance** and intelligence operations and take supplies or airmen where they need to be. Communication is key at all times. CSOs oversee any information that comes into or goes out of the aircraft.

This combat systems officer is directing rescue aircraft from the roof of a flooded building.

THE NEW WARFARE

In combat today, the electronic warfare officer, a type of CSO, has become very important. These officers work with electronic systems to disrupt things such as enemy communications and **radar**. They also defend against enemy forces trying to do the same thing. Electronic warfare officers do the research and planning for any of these missions. They work on electronic warfare aircraft, such as the U.S. Air Force's F-35 Joint Strike Fighter. A specially trained CSO operates the aircraft's built-in systems that can track aircraft, **intercept** communications, and more.

REMOTELY PILOTED AIRCRAFT

Air Force missions sometimes use aircraft without pilots in the cockpit. These are Remotely Piloted Aircraft (RPA). Today's RPAs are not just drones for gathering intelligence. The Air Force can use them for military strikes and to protect troops on the ground. CSOs use satellite communications to direct RPA missions.

Air Force CSOs navigate and oversee remotely piloted aircraft.

Captain Holly Mapel:
LIVING THE DREAM

For as long as she can remember, Captain Holly Mapel wanted to be in the U.S. Air Force. Her father and other family members served in the military, and Mapel wanted to follow in their footsteps. More than anything, she wanted to fly. Just months after finishing high school, Mapel enlisted in the U.S. Air Force. She could not wait to get started on her dream career.

Your FRONTLINE Career

Is Being a CSO for You?

Sounds Great
- Being part of a wide range of missions
- Working with the latest electronics and weapons systems
- Having a central role in planning and mission command
- Pilot and navigation training

Things to Think About
- Long deployments
- Must be very focused and disciplined
- Responsible for important, life-and-death decisions
- A lot of computer-based work

Mapel took a different route to becoming a CSO. Her first job in the Air Force was working as a flight equipment technician. Flight equipment technicians have to make sure that the supplies on a flight are working properly and are safe to use. The supplies include parachutes and helmets, as well as survival kits. Equipment technicians ensure that the airmen on a mission have everything they need for any situation.

After working on the ground for seven years, Mapel decided to make a change. Her work with the Special Operations Command crew had inspired her to go back to school to earn a degree. Doing this was not easy, because she had to work while she was studying.

After graduating, Mapel started her training at the Officer Training School, and she became a CSO.

For two years, Mapel worked as an electronic warfare officer with a Special Operations squadron. She was the officer in charge of planning, navigation, and making sure that areas were safe for dropping people or supplies. But she wanted another challenge, so she moved to the Commando II.

The Air Force uses this aircraft for covert refueling missions and to drop or collect Special Ops forces into hostile territories. Mapel's training included learning how to use a new radar system that enabled her to find information about the land and weather and create maps of hostile areas. The system also allows pilots to fly aircraft closer to the ground without being detected.

Captain Mapel has come a long way from her days as a supply technician. She now has two jobs that she loves. She leads a group of airmen and civilians in testing operations and works as a CSO. With hard work and training, Mapel's dreams of an exciting, challenging flying career came true.

In addition to being a CSO, Mapel is qualified to test equipment and weapons on many different aircraft.

AIR TRAFFIC CONTROL

Different types of military aircraft take off and land all over the world. Air traffic controllers (ATCs), or aerospace control officers, as they are known in the Canadian Armed Forces, make sure that everything happens safely, both on the ground and in the air. This means keeping thousands of airmen and civilians from harm. It also involves protecting aircraft and equipment worth many millions of dollars each.

LEARNING THE BASICS

ATCs start their careers with basic training. After basic training, the next step is taking a specialized operator course and earning an aviation certificate. Trainees learn about aircraft, radar, and how to use charts and maps. Training also includes learning the correct words and procedures that allow controllers to communicate quickly and clearly with the aircrew and other controllers. ATCs go on to work in control towers and radar control rooms. They may also be frontline airmen called combat controllers.

Airmen in the radar control room guide many aircraft through thousands of miles of airspace above both land and water.

In the tower, air traffic controllers have a view in all directions as they direct fighter aircraft.

DIRECTING TRAFFIC

ATCs know what is in the air and on the ground at all times. They direct aircraft takeoffs and landings, and they use radar to track flights. Computers help determine aircraft altitudes (height above sea level), speeds, and directions, and ATCs have to understand this information and how to use it. Pilots depend on them for detailed information about flight plans and the weather. ATCs and pilots use radio equipment to communicate, and ATCs keep records of everything. Sometimes, communications break down, or an aircraft has a malfunction and has to return to base. Other emergencies might happen on the ground, such as an oil spill. ATCs have to alert emergency services, such as fire and ambulance, and calmly direct or redirect flights as necessary.

IN THE CONTROL ROOM

ATCs have to work well under pressure. They must be able to handle a lot of information at the same time. Successful controllers are excellent communicators, and they work well as a team. ATCs must be willing to work in different parts of the world. This can be exciting, but it also takes people far away from family.

TSgt Thomas Bauhs:

SAVING LIVES

Using the darkness of night as cover, the U.S. forces slipped into hostile territory in Afghanistan on June 1, 2014. U.S. Air Force Technical Sergeant (TSgt) Thomas Bauhs, a combat controller, was deployed with an Army Special Operations Forces unit. Another combat controller, a pararescue airman, and a team of Afghan National forces joined them. Their mission was to clear the Taliban-controlled area and make it safe.

Your FRONTLINE Career

Is Being a Technical Sergeant for You?

Sounds Great
• Being a critical person on the front line
• Deployed all over the world
• All-around training, including survival skills
• Working with advanced weaponry and equipment

Things to Think About
• Operating within hostile, enemy territories
• Working with different military teams whenever and wherever needed
• Extremely physical demands
• Sometimes work alone in remote areas

At first, the allied team faced little enemy fire, and the forces spread out. But by early afternoon, Taliban forces surrounded them. Bauhs and the Army ground force commander were on a rooftop. For six hours, Bauhs and the commander faced heavy machine-gun fire and grenades. They launched grenades and rifle fire in return, trying to take cover behind a wall on the roof. Bauhs used the cover to prepare and control an air strike. Two F16 fighter planes were waiting for instructions. Just then, a blast threw Bauhs off his feet. He had just managed to get to his feet when another blast hit. This one struck the wall above Bauhs's head. In seconds, the rooftop wall collapsed, and hard mud struck Bauhs on the head. The blast made his eardrums burst, and he could not hear at first. The air was also thick with smoke. Bauhs asked the other combat controller to direct the F16 bomb strikes, so he could tend to the Army commander. When Bauhs reached the commander, he saw that the attack had killed him. Bauhs radioed for help.

Combat controllers such as Bauhs direct air strikes and medical aircraft through constant radio communication.

Other soldiers on the ground were wounded, and Bauhs started organizing a medical evacuation. He directed the helicopter to a safe landing area. Bauhs needed to make sure that the helicopter could land, take on wounded soldiers, and leave again. The Taliban fire did not stop. Bauhs coordinated more close air strikes to suppress the enemy attack. Meanwhile, he controlled the evacuation of other teammates. All this time, he was struggling with a severe head injury.

The fighting on June 1 lasted 12 hours. Bauhs's actions helped to save lives and clear the area according to the original mission. In 2015, Bauhs received the Bronze Star Medal with Valor. The medal honors a military person who has shown great heroism in combat.

BEHIND THE FRONT LINE

Missions can succeed or fail depending on the people behind the scenes. The U.S. Air Force has more than 200 different careers to choose from. Some of them involve missions and aircraft, while others make sure that all the Air Force bases and systems run smoothly. Thousands of technicians, computer experts, and other professionals work to maintain and repair aircraft, manage the airfields, and much more.

COMBAT PREP

The Air Force does not go into combat without planning. Many people are involved before and during any conflict. For example, intelligence officers collect and analyze information, such as the location of enemy aircraft. Many of these officers have foreign language skills. Fusion analysts are enlisted airmen who also work in intelligence. They figure out if information is valuable or not, and they also identify immediate threats, such as enemy approaches. Logistic planners make sure that people and equipment are organized, so that missions are successful.

Air force medics are on hand to help in emergency situations all over the world.

CYBER EXPERTS

Advanced computer systems enable the Air Force to run operations, interfere with enemy plans, and gather intelligence. In 2019, the U.S. Air Force created a special cyber unit to protect and defend the country in cyberspace. Cyber systems operators are enlisted airmen who specialize in designing and maintaining computer systems.

WHAT'S THE RIGHT JOB?

There are many different careers in the Air Force. If people enjoy mechanics and working with their hands, they may choose to repair and maintain aircraft. For others, high-tech science is more interesting. Air Force physicists and engineers work with lasers, nuclear weapons, and other advanced technology.

KEEPING THINGS MOVING

The Air Force owns billions of dollars' worth of aircraft as well as ground vehicles and equipment. These must all be organized and tracked. Material management airmen are supply specialists that ensure everything is where it needs to be. Meanwhile, many people make sure that the aircraft and their onboard systems are working as they should. The different parts of an aircraft need specialized attention. Technicians work on the electric and electronic systems. They maintain and repair engine controls, for example. Other technicians maintain radar and communications systems. Some jobs are very specialized. An aircraft **egress systems** technician is responsible for the emergency systems on an aircraft. If a pilot needs to escape in an emergency, these systems must be working properly.

Weapons mechanics safely install, remove, and maintain aircraft ammunitions.

LYDIA KAMPS:

PROBLEM-SOLVER

Seeing an Air Force jet up close for the first time was a thrill that Senior Airman Lydia Kamps will always remember. Kamps was attending a four-day, Women Soar You Soar AirVenture camp for girls in grades 9 to 12. At the camp, Kamps also saw an air show and took a welding class. She heard stories from female aviators and met many of them. Listening to the stories inspired Kamps to pursue a career in aviation.

Your FRONTLINE Career

Is Being an Avionics Technician for You?

Sounds Great

- Working with state-of-the-art aircraft systems
- Hands-on, electronic work
- Enlisted airman job that does not require a degree
- Essential job to keep aircraft operating safely

Things to Think About

- Often involves shift work, including night shifts
- Working outside or in an aircraft hangar
- May be deployed at an overseas base
- Does not take part in missions

Kamps did not join the Air Force right away. After high school, she got her pilot's certificate and worked as an electrician. In 2017, she joined the Air Force. Kamp's background as an electrician was helpful for becoming an avionics technician. The job is a crucial one because avionics technicians maintain all the electronic systems on board an aircraft. After training at a base in Texas, Kamps moved to another base in Arizona. Today, she works on fighter jets such as the F-16, just like the aircraft that caught her attention in high school.

The pilots who fly the fighter aircraft depend on the work that Kamps does. Before any aircraft goes out, Kamps checks that the radar, weapons, radio systems, and more are working. If something is wrong, Kamps can fix it. Kamps works in the United States, but avionics technicians can be based all over the world. They work in aircraft hangars, and the hours can be very long.

However, each day presents a challenge and a different problem to solve. Aircraft systems are complex, and technicians have to keep up to date with any new aircraft the Air Force buys.

In her position, Kamps has the opportunity to think about other jobs she might like to do. The Air Force supports its airmen by offering help with education costs and flexible working schedules. Kamps may get a degree and become an Air Force pilot. She also gives talks to high school girls about what the Air Force can offer and careers in the U.S. Air Force. She knows how important it is for young girls to see that women can succeed in a military career, so she uses her story to inspire others, just as other women inspired her years before.

Kamps (shown above, center left) also works as a volunteer with the White Ropes program, in which Air Force recruits volunteer their time to help people in local communities.

COULD YOU BE ON THE FRONT LINE?

Do you have what it takes to be in the Air Force? Here are some of the key things you need to think about if you are serious about signing up.

EDUCATION

To get into the U.S. or Canadian Air Force, you need a high school diploma or GED. You can take courses in high school that might help you in your career. For example, science courses, including computing or technology classes, may be useful. If you want to be an officer, you will have to earn a university or college degree.

FAMILY

Is the Air Force the place for you? Talk to your family about why you want to join. Are you ready to be far away from family and friends? If you want to be a pilot, you have to commit to ten years of service. Other careers need commitments of four or six years.

PHYSICAL FITNESS

All armed forces require a high degree of physical fitness. When you sign up, you will have to take tests to see if you are fit enough for basic training. Prepare for this test by keeping active and eating well. Be aware that basic training will be tough. Age is something to consider, too. For most Air Force careers, you must be at least 17 (with a parent's permission) and no older than 39 to begin your training.

MENTALLY FIT

Many Air Force jobs are highly stressful, even if they are not on the front line. Are you good at handling many jobs at once? Many Air Force careers mean juggling tasks and staying focused at the same time. You have to be prepared to keep going, even if you feel exhausted.

TEAM PLAYER

Joining the Air Force means being part of a team. It means working with your squadron but also with other units. Do you play any team sports? Team members rely on each other to win. Airmen also rely on each other. This is crucial on the front line, especially. Get some experience working and playing sports with others.

WHAT JOB?

The Air Force offers careers in all different areas, from working on aircraft to flying them. You may want to be an Air Force doctor or medic. You may like working with money and accounts and choose to be in finance. Also think about whether you want to be an active duty airman or a reserve. There are plenty of opportunities in both.

LEARN MORE

To find out more about life in the Air Force and what it offers, go online (see links on page 31) or contact a local **recruiter**. A recruiter will be able to answer all the questions you may have.

CAPT RICH MEADOWS
PHYN
NASO CO

WARNING

GLOSSARY

allied Countries or groups that agree to work together

aptitude To have a natural ability to do something

ballistic missile A rocket-propelled weapon that shoots through the sky and at long distances before exploding

bases Military facilities

biological Describes germ warfare, which is a system of using dangerous and deadly bacteria and viruses to attack civilians

chain of command A series of positions arranged from most important or powerful to least

civilian An ordinary person

commissioned Appointed

compound A group of several buildings where people live and work, often surrounded by a wall or fence

conventional Usually used; in weaponry, arms that are not nuclear

counterterrorism Acting against terrorist actions

cyberspace The world of computers and the Internet

deployed Sent on a mission or tour of duty

disciplined A way of behaving that involves following rules and the ability to keep working on something difficult

discrimination Treating people who belong to a particular group unfairly

egress system The parts of an aircraft that allow a pilot to quickly escape, such as an ejection seat

electronic warfare Military action that involves the use of the electromagnetic spectrum, such as signals, radio, radar, and infrared

enlisted Joined a branch of the military

ethics Rules of behavior related to what is right or wrong

evacuation Removal from a dangerous place

grenades Small, handheld bombs

hostile Threatening and dangerous

humanitarian crisis When a huge amount of suffering is caused to people, for example, when people become homeless and are without food and water because of a disaster, such as a flood

intelligence Secret information

intercept listen in secretly to another's communication; also to prevent someone from continuing to a destination

meteorologists Scientists who study the weather

meteorology The study of weather patterns

navigation To find one's way from one place to another, especially in unknown areas

nuclear Related to weapons that use deadly and destructive nuclear energy

pararescue Operation involving rescue teams who parachute from an aircraft

personnel The people who work for an organization or company

piracy Attacking and stealing from a ship at sea

precision Accurate and exact

radar A machine that can pick up the position of a person or object using radio waves

rank The job level achieved by an officer

reconnaissance To secretly find out about an enemy

recruiter A person in the military who helps people enlist

satellites Devices in space used for communication

security Protection against enemy danger or threat

simulated When something looks and/or behaves like something else

stationed Sent or based, where soldiers stay when they are in battle

surveillance Watching someone or something to prevent an attack

tactical Relating to military actions in plans, procedures, and operations

Taliban A violent religious group that wants to rule in Afghanistan

virtual reality An artificial world of sights and sounds created by a computer

LEARNING MORE

Discover more about the Air Force and careers on the front line.

BOOKS

Mitchell, P. P. *Join the Air Force* (U.S. Armed Forces). Gareth Stevens, 2017.

Russo, Kristin J. *Surprising Facts about Being an Air Force Airman.*
   Edge Books, 2017.

Sherman, Jill. *U.S. Air Force* (Serving Our Country). Amicus, 2019.

Sneddon, Robert. *Air Force* (Defend and Protect). Gareth Stevens, 2016.

Hansen, Ole Steen. *Modern Military Aircraft.* Crabtree Publishing, 2003.

WEBSITES

Learn about the U.S. Air Force Academy and what it takes to apply at:
www.academyadmissions.com

See what careers the U.S. Air Force has to offer and what training is needed
at the Force's site:
www.airforce.com

Find out more about the Royal Canadian Air Force at:
https://forces.ca/en/how-to-join

To learn more about Royal Canadian Air Force careers in particular, visit:
https://forces.ca/en/about-us/air

There are specialized training programs for Indigenous peoples in Canada.
Learn more at:
https://forces.ca/en/programs-for-indigenous-peoples/#cfaept

INDEX

ABOUT THE AUTHOR

Cynthia O'Brien has written books on careers, history, science, animals, and many other subjects. Her father served for a time in the Royal Canadian Air Force, and she found writing about careers in the Air Force fascinating, especially learning about how many different, exciting opportunities exist within this service.